Project Management

Cheat Sheet

Muhammad Zeeshan Ali, PMP, PMI-ACP

Saqib Javed John, PMP, PMI-ACP, ITIL

Publications
2020

All inquiries should be addressed to (e-mail): publications@ogmcs.com

First Printing: 2021

ISBN: 9798713949631

OGMC Publications
publications.ogmcs.com

Ordering Information:
Special discounts are available on quantity purchases by corporations, associations, educators, and others. For details, contact the publisher at the above listed address.

Authors' Profile

Muhammad Zeeshan Ali

PMP, PMI-ACP

Saqib Javed John

PMP, PMI-ACP, ITIL

Author of multiple books and numerous articles elaborating new dimensions of Agile framework and Traditional Project Management along with his work on Performance Management, PMO, Leadership, Team Building and Personal Motivation. He is best known for designing first of its kind "Performance Measurement Matrix" to calculate number-based performance indicators and scoring for both Software Engineering Individuals and Teams. Zeeshan is a great advocate and promoter of adaptation of Agile Methodologies, Processes and Team Skill building.

Zeeshan has over 18 years of experience of managing 100+ mid-large scale, high visibility projects in both Public and Private sectors. Experienced in managing several significant projects simultaneously and with team spread over different geo-locations.

Zeeshan has Degrees in Project Management (MS) and Computer Sciences (BS). He has been certified as a Project Management Professional (PMP) and Agile Certified Professional (PMI-ACP) by Project Management Institute (PMI), USA.

Saqib is one of the founding members and Managing Director of Organizational Governance Management Consultants (OGMC). He has professional expertise of more than 18 years of working on enterprise projects in various business domains ranging from functional organization to projectized organization.

Saqib has immense experience in developing and managing human behavior, process engineering and optimization, risk management, conflict management, performance maturity audits and policy making. This is one of the reasons he is relatable to readers of Business and management professions. He is the best known for his rapid-learning techniques and easy methods of practical implementations. He also has contributed to many anthologies. His work is helping thousands of students, teachers and professionals.

Saqib is MS (IT), certified "Project Management Professional" (PMP) and "Agile Certified Practitioner" (ACP) from Project Management Institute (PMI) USA. He is also certified in "Information Technology Infrastructure Library" (ITIL) from Exin UK, "Sun Certified Java Programmer" (SCJP) and "Sun Certified Web Component Developer" (SCWCD) from Sun Microsystems USA.

Contents

1.0　Key Points for PMP Exam

1.1 Few General Points

1. PMP is framework while waterfall is a methodology
2. Simplicity = to unfold the undone work
3. **Standard** is a formal document that describes established norms, methods, process and procedures.
4. **Product:** is sequential, non-overlapping, and last retired.
5. **Project** is temporary having definite beginning and end and always produce a unique product, result or service.
6. **Operations** are permanent.
7. **Prototyping** is working module before Actual to get early feedback.
8. Subdividing work packages into more manageable components called "**Activities**" which shows the efforts required to complete work package.
9. Rolling Wave Planning = Progressive Elaboration Planning
10. **Heuristic**; Rules for which no formula exist usually derived through Trial and Error
11. **Value Engineering**; To try more out of the project in every possible way
12. **Budgeted at Completion (BAC)**; how much originally expected the project to cost
13. The **Higher Standard Deviation** is, the more diverse data points are

14. The most common example of Co-Location is the "**War Room**"

15. Project can be broken down into **Sub Project** and that can be broken down further

16. **Program** contains only related projects but **Portfolio** can contain unrelated projects

17. If a company is doing one particular batch of work each year then will be called as **"Program'**

18. Transition from one phase to another phase such as Design to Manufacturing is called **"Technical Transfer or Handoff"**

19. Developing in steps and continuing by increments is called **Progressive Elaboration**

20. **"Special Cause"** may also be referred as **"Assignable Cause"**

21. **Deming's formula** of continuous improvement is **Plan-Do-Check-Act**

22. Minimum information that **Issue-Log** should contain is the "Owner Name" and "Target Resolution Date"

23. **Manage & Control Project Work** gives you insight of the Project Health

24. **Final Acceptance** cannot be informal

25. **Coercive Power** is an example of Gentle Threat "if you don't do, I will tell your Functional Manager"

26. **Acceptable Variance** will tend to decrease as the project progresses

27. The number of the **activity attribute** varies by application area

28. Estimating and Forecasting future outcome based on the historical data called "**Time Series Method**"

29. Impact of the **Project** usually do not ends with the Project end

30. **Unplanned Trainings** include observations, conversations and Project Management appraisals

31. To know the **Failure Reasons**, review Audit Report related to the work area

32. **Precise** means values are clustered and **Accuracy** means values are close to the actual value

33. **Precision** is Consistency while **Accuracy** is Correctness

34. **Do not Bid** if you are not expert in the required filed/area.

35. **Manual Forecasting** is the best way to forecast **ETC**

36. **Decision Tree** will not be used when Future scenarios are known

1.2   Project Management Process Groups

1. **Process Groups:** Initiation, Planning, Execution, Monitoring & Control, Closing

2. **Knowledge Areas:** Integration, Scope, Time, Cost, Quality, HR, Communication, Risk and Procurement, Stakeholders.

3. Below are the high level outputs of each process group.

Process Group	Output
Initiation	Project Charter
Planning	Project Management Plan
Execution, Monitoring & Control	Acceptable Deliverables
Closing	Archive of Project Documentation

4. Initiation = Pre-Planning

5. Two processes should not overlap unless project is cancelled i.e. "**Initiation**" and "**Closing**"

6. Verifying a Product meets specifications is a part of **Closing Process Group**

7. Phase Gate, Phase Exist and Kill Point are the Valid Terms for **Closing the Phase.**

8. All processes of "**Planning**" have one common output i.e. "Project Document Update"

9. All processes of "**Execution**" and "**M&C**", have few common outputs i.e. "Project Document Update", "PM Plan Update", "Org. Process Assets Update" and "Change Request"

10. In M&C process group, "Scope", "Time" and "Cost" has one common output i.e. "Work Performance Measurements" while "Quality" has out as "Quality Control Measurements"

11. **Processes and Procedures** are improved in result of Audit

12. Process which run again and again during the life cycle of the project is called **"Iterative"**

13. In a Process always you go forward and then you keep one step back to review what you have done

14. **"Execution"** process group usually takes the largest effort in the Project

15. OPM3, CMMI and Malcolm-Baldrige are the **Process Improvement methods** but no the TQM

16. Early Termination procedures are also written as part of **"Close Project or Close Phase"** process

1.3 Project Management and Project Management Plan

1. **Project Management Plan** is singed off by Project Manager, Functional Manager and Project Sponsor

2. **Schedule** is one of the most visible and important part of the **Project Management Plan**

3. **Project Management** is an application of skills, knowledge, tools and techniques

4. **Project Management Life Cycle** remains always same i.e. I-P-E-MC-C

5. **Project Life Cycle** varies as per the nature of project and industry.

6. **"Mushroom Project Management"** by keeping everything buried under the carpet.

7. **Successful Project** means meeting Customer's, Sponsor's and Stakeholders expectations

1.4 Diagraming Tools and Techniques

1. **Affinity Diagram** allows a large number of ideas into different groups for further review and analysis

2. "Effect" is on head of the **Fishbone Diagram**

3. **RAM** diagram shows the relationship between work packages and Project Team Members

4. **Cause and Effect Diagram** also known as Ishikawa Diagram or Fishbone Diagram, shows how the various factors linked with potential problem or effect.

5. **Scatter Diagram** is used to show Quality Impacts

6. **Scatter Diagram** is the relationship between two variables or the relationship between dependent and independent variables are plotted; the closer points are to diagonal line, the more closely related they are.

7. **Tornado Diagram** is used to see the relative importance of the variables

1.5 Analysis Tools and Techniques

1. **Root Cause Analysis** includes, "Problem Identification", "Discovery of underlying causes" and development of Preventive Actions

2. **"Expected Monetary Value Analysis"** are used to calculate Financial Impact

3. **What-if Analysis;** this technique analyze multiple scenarios to find the best way to align the plan with reality.

4. **What If Analysis (**(Monte Carlo Analysis) are used to determine how to deal with unexpected situation

5. **Process Analysis** includes Root Cause Analysis

6. **Earn Value Analysis** can be presented in Tabular Form as well as S-Curve

7. "**Failure Mode and Effect Analysis**" used to find impact of Failures.

8. **"System Breakdown"** is not a Product Analysis Technique

9. **Process Analysis** required also to identify non-value added activities

10. **Regression Analysis** is used to forecast future project performance

11. **Reserve Analysis** are performed during "Estimate Cost" process

12. For Root Cause Analysis two techniques can be used, Cause & Effect Diagram and Why-Why and How-How diagram

1.6   Precedence and Critical Path

1. A project can have more than one critical path
2. "Float" is also known as "Slack"
3. **CPM** (Critical Path Method) either has zero or negative Float Value
4. **Float** is that for how much time an activity can slip without effecting the critical path, so an item on critical path has "**Zero Float**"
5. **Negative Float;** if an activity end before its scheduled start date and it will be the clear indication that there is some serious issue with the schedule.
6. **Backward Pass;** method for calculating Late Start and Late Finish date
7. **Forward Pass;** method for calculating Early Start and Early Finish date
8. Precedence Diagramming Method (**PDM**) is also known as Activity on Node (**AON**)
9. **PDM** is used in **CPM** (Critical Path Method) to get **PSND** (Project Schedule Network Diagram)
10. Arrow Diagramming Method (**ADM**) is also known as Activity on Arrow (**AOA**)

11. **PSND** (Project Schedule Network Diagram) is not the schedule

12. **ADM** has only one relation that is F – S

13. Critical Path without Resource Constraint called **CPM** (Critical Path Method).

14. Critical Path with Resource Constraint called **CCM** (Critical Chain Method).

15. **CCM** it provides the way to view and manage uncertainty and resources during the project schedule.

16. **CPM** is used to calculate ES (Early Start), EF (Early Finish), LS (Late Start), and LF(Late Finish) dates by using Forward and Backward Pass Analysis

17. **CPM** is used to calculate project finish date and to find activities which can slip and also those activities which can't slip, called **High Risk Activities**.

18. **Critical Path Method (CPM)** is a combination of activities and if any one delayed then it will delay the finish date of the project.

19. In CPM, buffer is added at activity level while in CCM buffer is added as lum-sum

20. **Critical Activities** are those which exist on Critical Path.

21. **Total Float** is the positive difference between early and late dates i.e. ((ES-LS) and (EF-LF))

22. **Total Float** of each activity on critical path will be **Zero** that is called **Zero Float**.

23. **Lead** allow an acceleration of successor activity

24. **Activity duration estimates** should not include any Lead or Lag value

25. "**Lead**" is the jump-start to another activity while "**Lag**" is the waiting period between the activities

26. **Lag;** Delay in successor Activity

27. One Activity should mapped back to only one work package; however, work packages can have more than one activities belong to it.

28. **Additional Buffer** is also known as Feeding Buffer.

29. **Feeding Buffers** protects Critical Chain from slippages.

30. Preceding = Predecessor

31. F – S is the most common precedence relation used

1.7 Performance Baseline and Earn Value Management

1. The most important output of the Project Management framework is the "**Deliverables**" and 2nd most important is "**Work Performance Information (WPI)**"

2. **Team Performance Assessments** are down during Team Development Process.

3. **Performance Reports** include information on Scope, Time, Cost and Quality

4. Cost Performance Baseline = BAC (Budgeted at Completion)

5. **Actual Costs** are measured against Cost Performance Baseline.

6. **Cost Performance Index** is widely used to forecast Project Cost at Completion

7. In **EVM** technique, Cost Performance Baseline is referred to "Performance Measurement Baseline"

8. Central Point of doing overall Performance Measurement is "**Control Account**"

9. **Employment Performance Review** is not the Enterprise Environmental Factor

10. "Econometric Model" is used for future project performance based on assumptions

11. Performance of Individual Team member should not be the part of **"Final Project Report"**

12. **EVM methodology;** used to forecast future performance based on past performance

13. **EVM** is a method for Performance Measurement and it integrates Scope, Time and Cost and the principal of EVM can be applied to all industries.

14. **EVM** includes EV, PV and AC and based on these values; Variance, Performance index and Forecasting can be calculated.

15. **PV** = Value of the work Planned

16. **EV** = Value of the work Performed

17. **AC** = Actual Cost incurred for the completed work and will not have any upper limit

18. **Present Value (PV)** does not factor in Cost

19. CPI > 1 (Over Budget, Cost overrun) …….Bad

20. SPI < 1 (Behind Schedule, Time overrun) ……Bad

21. TCPI < 1 …..Good

1.8 Quality Controls (Charts)

1. **Run Chart** is similar to Control Chart but without limits shows the history and variation of pattern.

2. Runs Charts = shows Trends

3. **Control Charts** are also known as "**Rule of Seven**"; Upper & Lower limits are based on requirements of Contract, and will be called "Out of Control" if seven consecutive data points are above or below the mean.

4. **Flow Chart** is a graphical representation of a process

5. "**Control Chart**" is the tool used in both Plan Quality and Control Quality

6. Bar Chart that reports for control and manage communication, is called **Hammock** activity.

7. Pareto Chart is kind of Histogram showing frequency sequence Top to Bottom

8. Pareto Chart is also known as 80/20 Rule or Pareto Law, means 80% of problems comes from 20% of causes.

9. Run Charts are used for Trend Analysis.

10. Pareto Diagram helps the management team to quantify and categorize the defects

11. **Milestone chart** only represents the key events and can be used for high level project presentations.

1.9 Project Quality Management

1. **Perform QC** will determine the correctness of the deliverables

2. **"Perform QC"** is done before **"Verify Scope"**

3. **Quality Management Plan** tells that how the quality policy will be met

4. **Quality Matrix** tells how the quality will be measured

5. **Quality checklist** provides all steps and their sequence

6. **Quality** is not "Inspected in", infact its "Planned in" and "Build in"

7. **QA** is the Audit of Quality Requirements

8. **CoQ** is Cost of all efforts made to develop and maintain the quality during the project or product life cycle

9. **CoPQ; Cost of Poor Quality** (also called **Failure Cost**)

a. Internal CoPQ (found by Project Team)

b. External CoPQ (found by Customer)

10. **Quality Matrix** tells how quality control processes will measure and are used in Quality Control and Quality Assurance processes

11. **Quality Check list;** usually component specific and it is used to verify that set of required steps has been performed or not

12. **Statistical Sampling** is not the part of seven basic tools of Quality

13. Appropriate **Sampling** can often reduce the Cost of Quality Control

14. **TQM** applies for improvement in Processes and Results

1.10 Project Stakeholders Management

1. **Issue-Log** is used as Input to manage Stakeholder's Expectations

2. **Stakeholders** can be identified at any stage of the Project

3. Not all stakeholders should be treated equally on the Project

4. **Stakeholders** have maximum influence at the initial stage of the project

5. **"Salience Model"** shows stakeholders power based on Power, Urgency and Legitimacy

6. **"Low Power and Low Interest"** these kind of stakeholders only just need to monitor

7. "Power/Influence" grid and "Influence/Impact" grid along with Salience Model are the Legitimate models to **identify Stakeholders and their expectations**

8. **Stakeholders** are at all level exist with varying degree of Authority

1.11 Motivation Theories

1. **McGregor's Theory;**
   a. **X Managers**; who believe that constant supervision required to get desired results
   b. **Y Managers**; People are naturally self-motivated to do Good and need very little external motivation
2. **Herzberg (Motivation Hygiene Theory);** give those factors which motivate team at work.
3. **Contingency Theory;**
   a. **Leadership** (Task oriented or Relationship oriented)
   b. **Work Environment** (Stressful or Easy to Work)

1.12 Integrated Change Control & Configuration Management

1. Every change to the project weather requested or not, should be performed through **"Perform Integrated Change Control".**
2. **Contract Change Control System** is the part of Integrated Change Control
3. **Integrated Change Control Management** includes
   a. Change Request
   b. Configuration Management (and this further includes)

      i. Configuration Identification

     ii. Configuration Status Accounting

    iii. Configuration Verification and Audit

4.   "**Configuration Management System**" allows the Project Team to communicate with all stakeholders about approved and rejected changes

5.   **Configuration Control** is focused on both, specifications of Deliverables and Processes

6.   **Configuration Management** System is the Sub-Component of Project Management Information System

7.   **Adapting changes to Project Management Plan** is the part of "Direct and Manage Project Execution"

8.   **Change Control** can change the Product as well as the way its constructed

9.   To bring Future Results in line with Project Plan need **Corrective Actions**

1.13   Project Cost Management

1.   **Accuracy of Cost Estimates** will increase with the life of the Project.

2.   Cost of maintaining and supporting the Product is called **"Life Cycle Costing"**

3.   Relation of Cost and Risk, when Cost goes up then Risk, Stakeholder's influence and uncertainty goes down.

4. **Cost Benefit Ratio (CBR)** means Ratio of benefits to the cost

a. CBR = Selling Cost / Construction Cost

5. **Opportunity Cost** is the cost of other opportunities we missed by investing our money in one specific project. "As Dollar can be invested at one place at one time"

6. **Independent Estimates** are used to have intended Cost.

7. Profit Margin is not the part of "**Cost Estimations**"

8. If **Indirect Cost** required to add in estimates then it should be added either on Activity level or higher level

9. Both **Direct and Indirect** Cost should be considered while doing analysis for **Make or Buy** decision

10. Estimates will included only Direct Cost or would also include Indirect Cost, that decision will be taken in "**Estimate Cost**" Process

11. Cost of running PMO is also an example of "**Indirect Cost**"

12. If during testing, product is destroyed beyond use then Cost of such testing is usually classified as "**Appraisal Costs**"

13. **Cost of Quality** included all costs incurred over the life of a Product, it include cost of Conformance and Non-Conformance both

14. **Cost of Conformance** is the cost of Preventions or Appraisal, while **Cost of Non-Conformance** is the cost of Internal or External Failures

1.14 Procurement and Contracts

1. To make **Procurement File** is the part of Close Procurement Process which contains **"Indexed Contract Documents"**
2. **Procurement Management Plan** should be formal.
3. **Procurement Statement of Work** is written by Buyer and provided to prospective Seller.
4. **"Letter of Intent"** is not the part of Procurement Document.
5. **"Seller Proposal"** is not a common term/name related to Procurement Documents.
6. Huge difference between estimates figures could be because of deferent and ambiguous procurement Statements
7. **Legal Counsel** can be involved in all processes of Procurement Management
8. **Every Contract** must be closed
9. **Fixed Price Contact** is the highest risk to seller.
10. **Time and Material** contract is Good if Scope of work is not completely defined
11. In case of the constant change in Scope, **"Time & Material"** contract will be Good
12. **Contract Provisions** are generally considered as Constraints of the Project

13. **Contract** is the way to handle Non-Conforming deliverables

14. **Fixed Price** Contract, transfers the risk to Seller

15. "**Contract Administrator**" and "**Procurement Administrator**" are the valid terms

16. "**Cost Reimbursement Contract**" will be suited if scope is not clear and 100% chances exist of scope change

17. The method to evaluate the potential contractor is "**Evaluate Proposal**"

18. "**Time & Material**" and **Cost-Reimbursement** contracts have no definite end

19. Buyer's Cost Risk will be low in case of **Fixed Price Contract**

20. **Time and Material** is Hybrid Type of Contract/Agreement

21. In **Firm Fixed Price** Contract the Buyer must precisely specify the Service or Product to be procured

22. Fixed Price Incentive Fee is the **Point of Total Assumption,** here the seller has the most motivation to bring things to completion4

23. "**Quantitative Risk Analysis**" is not suitable for small scale and small budget projects

24. Risk related interviews are also conducted during "**Qualitative Risk Analysis**"

1.15 Estimates

1. **Analogous Analysis** are good for rough magnitude estimates based on Historic Projects
2. **Analogous Estimates** are used when limited information is available
3. **Analogous Estimates** are generally Less Accurate but quick & Less Cost
4. **Analogous Estimating** is also known as Top-Down estimates
5. **Parametric Estimates** are also known as Linear estimates

1.16 Project Resource Management

1. Cost of Human Resource is not the part of **"Resource Calendar"**
2. **Composite Resource Calendar** is Availability, Capability, and Skills of Human Resources
3. **Resource Breakdown Structure** is Hierarchal Structure of Resources
4. **Resource Leveling** is required when resources are over allocated
5. **Resources** may include both physical and human resource
6. **RBS** (Resource Breakdown Structure) is much similar to WBS as it's also graphical and hierarchal.

7. **RBS** can be linked with Project Cost and Organization Accounting System

8. Histogram is also known as Vertical Bar Chart or Column Chart that shows how often a particular variable status occurred

9. **Resource Calendar** is not an Enterprise Environmental factor

10. **Resource Histogram** is used for Resource Leveling and Project Staffing

11. **Resource Histogram** shows usage of resources in given period of time

1.17 Expert Judgment and Lesson Learned

1. In knowledge area "Integration", all process groups use only one Tool and Technique i.e. "Expert Judgment".

2. **Expert Judgment** is the richest source of data gathering

3. **Expert Judgment** is not the recommended tool for controlling schedule

4. Using trained people during collect requirements is the use of **Expert Judgment** or **Focus Group**

5. There is no substitute of **Expert Opinion**.

6. **Mistakes** are the potential assets if documented well in the form of the lesson learned

7. **Lesson Learned Document** is compiled throughout the Project but at minimum it should be updated at the end of the project

8. on lesson learned fall under the process of Direct & Manage Project Execution

1.18 Reserves

1. Reserves (Management or Contingency) are not the part of **"Project Cost Baseline"** but may be added in the Total Budget for the Project

2. **Contingency Reserves** are identified during the process "Determine Budget"

3. **Contingency Reserves** also known as Project Reserves and can apply to Schedule or Cost

4. **Contingency Reserves** are used for **"Anticipated but not for the Certain Events"**

5. **Management Reserves** are not the part of EVM calculations

1.19 Scope, Statement of Work and Business Case

1. **Collecting Requirements** includes both Project and Product Requirements

2. Training required should be mentioned in **"Requirements Documentations"**

3.   **Hidden participant** is used to uncover the large number of hidden requirements

4.   Defining Scope and providing Cost estimates are not the part of **Project Kick-Off Meeting.**

5.   **Business Case** contains Business needs and also Cost Benefit Analysis

6.   **Business Case** contains Business needs and also Cost Benefit Analysis

7.   For External Projects, SOW is not the part of Business Case, as it could be the part of RFI or RFP or Contract of Bid

8.   **SOW** does not refer to the Business Case

9.   **Project Scope** is measured against Project Management Plan and **Product Scope** is measured against Product Requirements

10.   Project Scope Statement also includes product acceptance criteria

11.   Completion of **Project Scope** can be validated against Project Management Plan

12.   **Crashing or Fast Tracking** does not reduce Scope

13.   **Requirements Traceability Matrix** helps tracing the Project Objectives, Scope and Strategy

14.   **Project Scope Statement** also contains the assumptions associated with the Project.

1.20 WBS

1. **WBS** is more closely related to **scope baseline** while activates are more closely related to **schedule baseline**.

2. **WBS** should be based on Deliverables as WBS is the key input for Time and Cost estimates.

3. Deliverables are decomposed into **work packages** and it is the **lowest** level of WBS.

4. **WBS** is the **information Hub** of the project

5. Product Work, Project Work and Project Management Work all three should be included in **WBS**

6. A high level project schedule of WBS components is called "**A Planning Package**"

7. **Activities** are the extension of WBS but not the part of WBS.

8. WBS component are also used for Cost Accounting

1.21 Project Charter

1. **Project Charter** is like a Birth Certificate of the Project

2. High Level Risks are listed in **Project Charter**

3. **Project Charter** is authorized by the Sponsor or Initiator, external to the Project Organization.

4. Business and Cost Benefit Analysis comes from requesting organization called "**Business Case**"; while developed from Performing Organization it will be called "**Charter**"

5. Govt. Standards and Industry Standards can be used as input to develop **Project Charter**

6. **Project Charter** will never be revised after Authorized

7. Business Case and Organization Process Assets can be used as an input to the **Project Charter**

8. Summary **milestone** schedule would normally the part of **Project Charter**

9. **Milestones** usually have no time associated with them

1.22 Risk Management

1. **Identify Risks** is an iterative process.

2. **Risk Identification** continuous throughout the Project

3. **Critical Path** tells that where the most of the project risks exist

4. **Mitigation** is the strategy which reduce the risk to the level it become acceptable

5. If the Project is closed due to high number of Risks then it will be an example of "**Risk Avoidance**"

6. Rating of "0" on Impact Scale is an indication of **Non-Conformance** of Risk and "1" is **Certainty**

7. **Risk** comes into play as soon as Project is Conceived

8. **Risks** may have one or more causes and one or more impacts as well

9. "**Quantitative Risk Analysis**" is not suitable for small scale and small budget project

10. Risk related interviews are also conducted during **"Qualitative Risk Analysis"**

11. Responses are also known as "Contingent Response Strategy" which are designed to use only if certain events occurs and are triggered by events such as "Missing Intermediate Milestones"

12. **"Avoiding"** is the change of Plan and Acceptance is no change in the plan.

13. **"Active Acceptance"** No Change in Plan and with Solution & Actions and **"Passive Acceptance"** No Change in Plan and without Solution and actions, but strategy will be documented in both the cases

1.23 Role and Responsibilities of Project Manager

1. **Project Manager** is responsible for Quality

2. **Project** cannot be authorized by the **Project Manager**

3. Highest priority for the **Project Manager** is to complete the Project as per defined Scope.

4. **Project Sponsor** could be one individual or group but Project Manager concern should be to have one sponsor only

5. Ultimate responsible of the Project Success is **"Project Manager"**

6. To manage virtual teams, **Project Manager** should be or need to be more Authoritative

7. In **Weak Matrix Organization**, Project Manager works as Project Coordinator

8. **Project Manager's** primary professional responsibility is towards all Stakeholders not only towards sponsor or performing organization

9. **Project Manager** is most likely to be involved in negotiation during Conduct Procurement process

10. **Project Manager's** role is integration of all process groups. Integration is like a glue which put bind everything together in a required order.

1.24 Abbreviations:

1. **OPM3:** Organizational Project Management Maturity Model

2. **PERT** stands for Program Evaluation and Review Technique also known as 3-Point estimates, weighted average of three estimates "Most-likely", "Pessimistic", "Optimistic"

3. **GERT:** stands for Graphical Evaluation and Review Technique

4. **RAM**: Responsibility Assignment Matrix

5. **RACI** (Ray-Cee): Responsibility, Accountability, Consult, Information

6. **CMMI:** Capability Maturity Model Integration

1.25 Project Team Management and Communication Management

1. **In Project Management;** communication should be always proactive.

2. **Project Management Team** is not external to the Project Team, because Project Management Team is the subset of Project Team

3. It is the responsibility of **Project Management Team** to maintain and ensure professionalism and follow ethical behavior

4. Most of the **Project Communication** is related to Project Performance and Performance Report

5. **Effective Project Manager** spends 90% of his time in communication and 50% of that in communicating with Project Team.

6. **"Written Communication"** is better for solving complex problem with Team.

7. If project has a very large audience then **"Pull Communication"** method will be appropriate

8. **Effective Communication**; Right Format, Right Time and Right Impact

9. **Efficient Communication**; is providing only information that is needed

10. Least amount of work done at "**Forming**" stage but team is at their "Best Behavior" on this stage

11. **Team Development Activities** are more effective at the start of the project

12. **Win-Win** rewards is the best choice for "**Team Building**"

13. **Team Building** can't be forced

14. To enforce **Ground Rules** is the share responsibility of all Project Team Members

15. **Ground Rules;** Formal or Informal but those are the boundaries of behavior on project

16. **Conflict** is not only individual issue, infact it's also a Team Issues

17. **Problem Solving** means resolving the conflict by Give and Take

18. **"Smoothing"** is not a long term solution for **Conflict Resolution**.

19. **Goal of Negotiation** is to reach Win-Win scenario between Buyer and Seller

20. **Negotiation** is the Technique used to bring Compromise

21. **Win-Lose** is also known as **Zero-Sum** and it's a type of Awards

22. **Reserve Time (Contingency)**; A Schedule Buffer to reduce Schedule Risk

2.0 Important Formulas

PV = Planned % completed x BAC

EV = Actual % completed x BAC

SV = EV − PV

CV = EV − AC

SPI = EV / PV

CPI = EV / AC

EAC (based on project performance) = BAC / CPI

EAC (based on BAC) = (BAC − EV) + AC

EAC = ETC + AC

ETC = EAC − AC

    Remaining Funds: BAC - AC

TCPI (based on BAC) = (BAC-EV) / (BAC-AC)

TCPI (based on EAC) = (BAC-EV) / (EAC-AC)

NPV: $FV / (1 + R)^n$

(R = Interest Rate, FV=Future Value, n=no. of time periods)

Communication Channels: n (n-1)/2

3-Point Estimates: (OP+(4xML)+PS) / 6

Range of Estimation Accuracy:

Definitive Estimates: -5% to +10%

Budget Estimates: -10% to +25%

Order of Magnitude: -25% to +75%

Standard Deviation: (Pessimistic – Optimistic) / 6

Variance = (Standard Deviation)^2

Early Finish (Forward Pass)**:** Early Start + Duration -1

Late Finish (Backward Pass)**:** Late Start + Duration -1

Duration: (EF – ES) + 1 or (LF – LS) + 1

Float: LS – ES or LF – EF

EMV (Expected Monitory Value) = Impact x Probability

PV is also known as BCWS (Budgeted Cost of Work Schedule)

EV is also known as BCWP (Budgeted Cost of Work Performed)

BCR; Higher is better

IRR; Higher is better

ROI; higher is better

CBR; lower is better

Payback Period; lower is better

3.0 Important Exam Tips

1. Usually people stop reading a day before exam but we must advise that please do not stop and keep revising the things as its very important to revise even those things which you know very well.

2. Don't invest time on such questions where you find very long descriptions or the questions giving you impression of difficulty and confusion. To manage such question, select any better option and put that question(s) on revision this way you can keep yourself away from going under the time pressure.

3. In order to give the right answer, you must be very sure about the three wrong answers, more or less this is the only way to give the confirmed right answer.

4. In Test/Exam room, you will get blank papers with couple of led pencils, use first 15 mins (i.e. Exam Tutorial Time) to write down the key points and formulas given in cheat sheet.

5. Must attempt the calculations based questions even if it takes little more time than the average because on such questions you will know there and then that your answer is right or wrong.

6. Keep concentrating on questions and don't eye much on the time clock, check your velocity only after 20 or 40 or 50 questions. It's a high speed exam, even seconds are important, analyzing the answering speed again and again will be time wasting and keep you under pressure.

7. Read well the question and all answers, before deciding the correct answer, if you are confused between 2 very close options then read the question again at least two times because usually solution of that ambiguity is hidden in question.

8. Try to reach at testing center one hour earlier than your exam time because testing center staff will also give you brief regarding exam rules etc. along with the few standard tips, listen to them even if you are already aware with rules/tips.

Other Books from OGMC Publications

Agile Practitioner
▶ Key Notes

Project Management
▶ Key Notes

Risk Management
▶ Key Notes

ITIL Foundation
▶ Key Notes

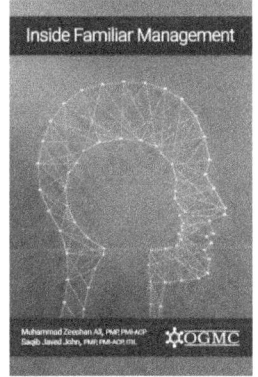

OGMC
Publications
PUBLICATIONS.OGMC.COM

Publications
PUBLICATIONS.OGMCS.COM